Colorful Clouds

Animal Coloring Book

Created By Mark Adamusik

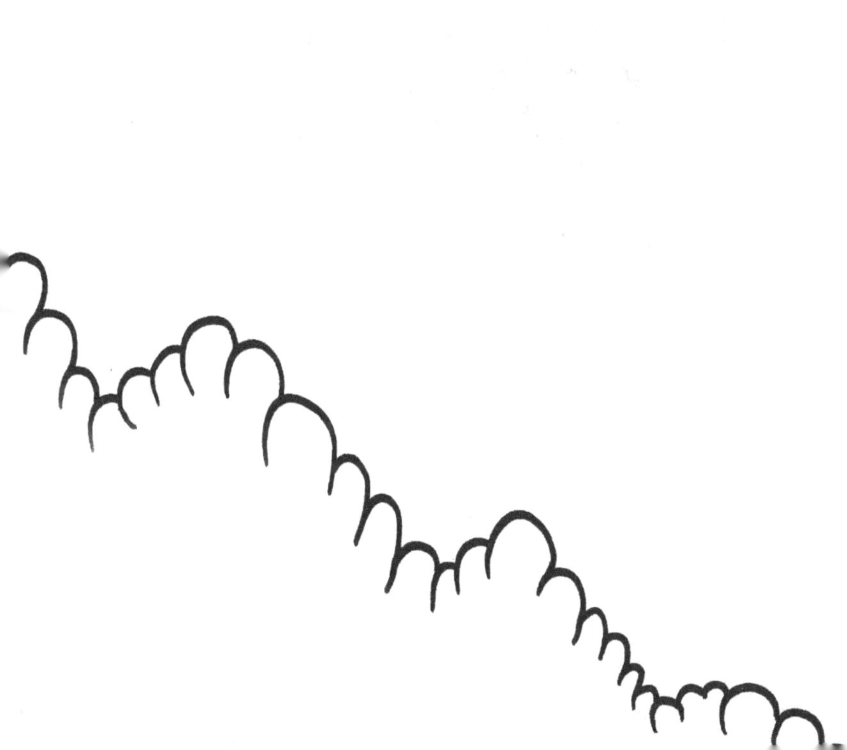

ISBN-13: 978-1547248452

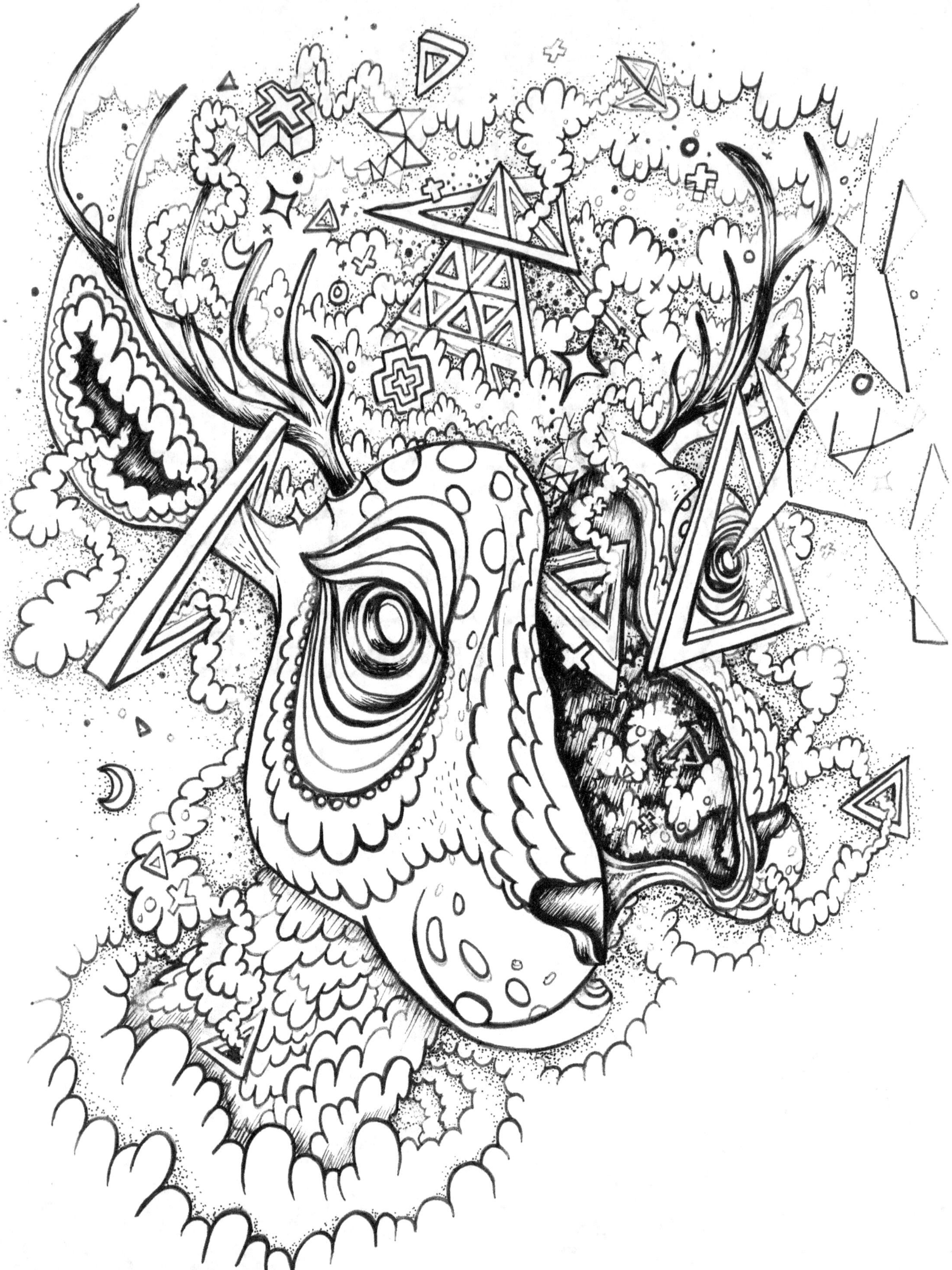

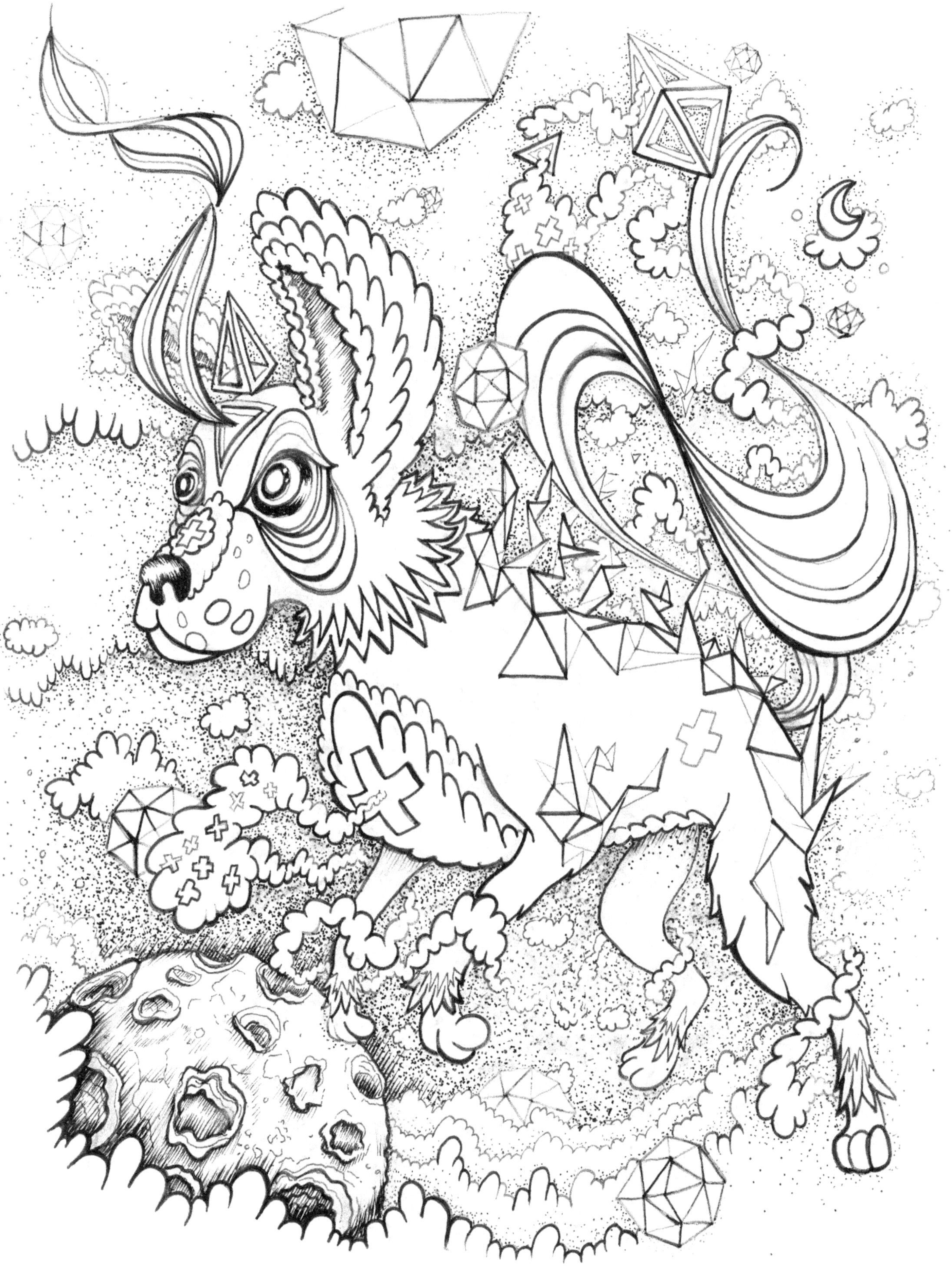

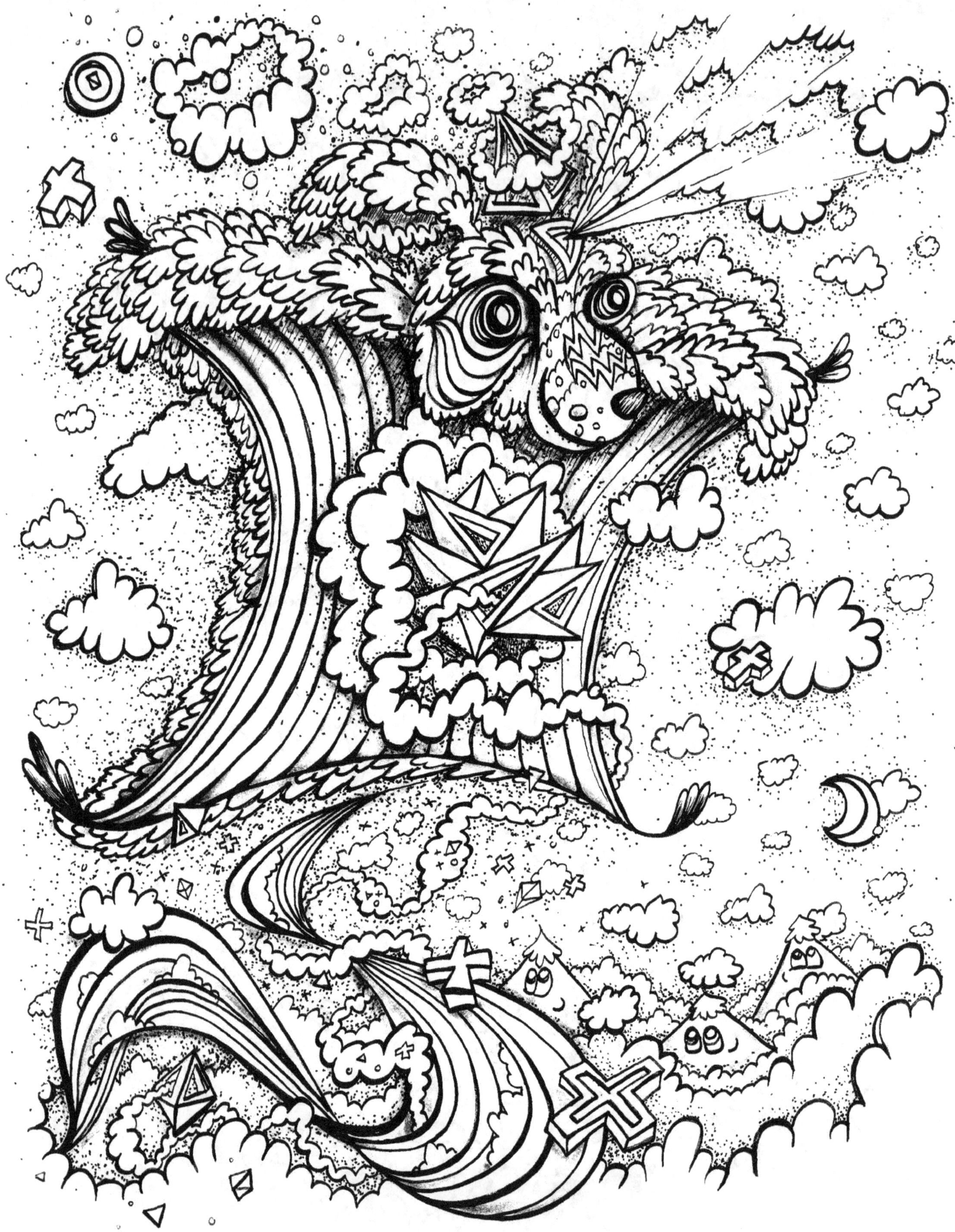

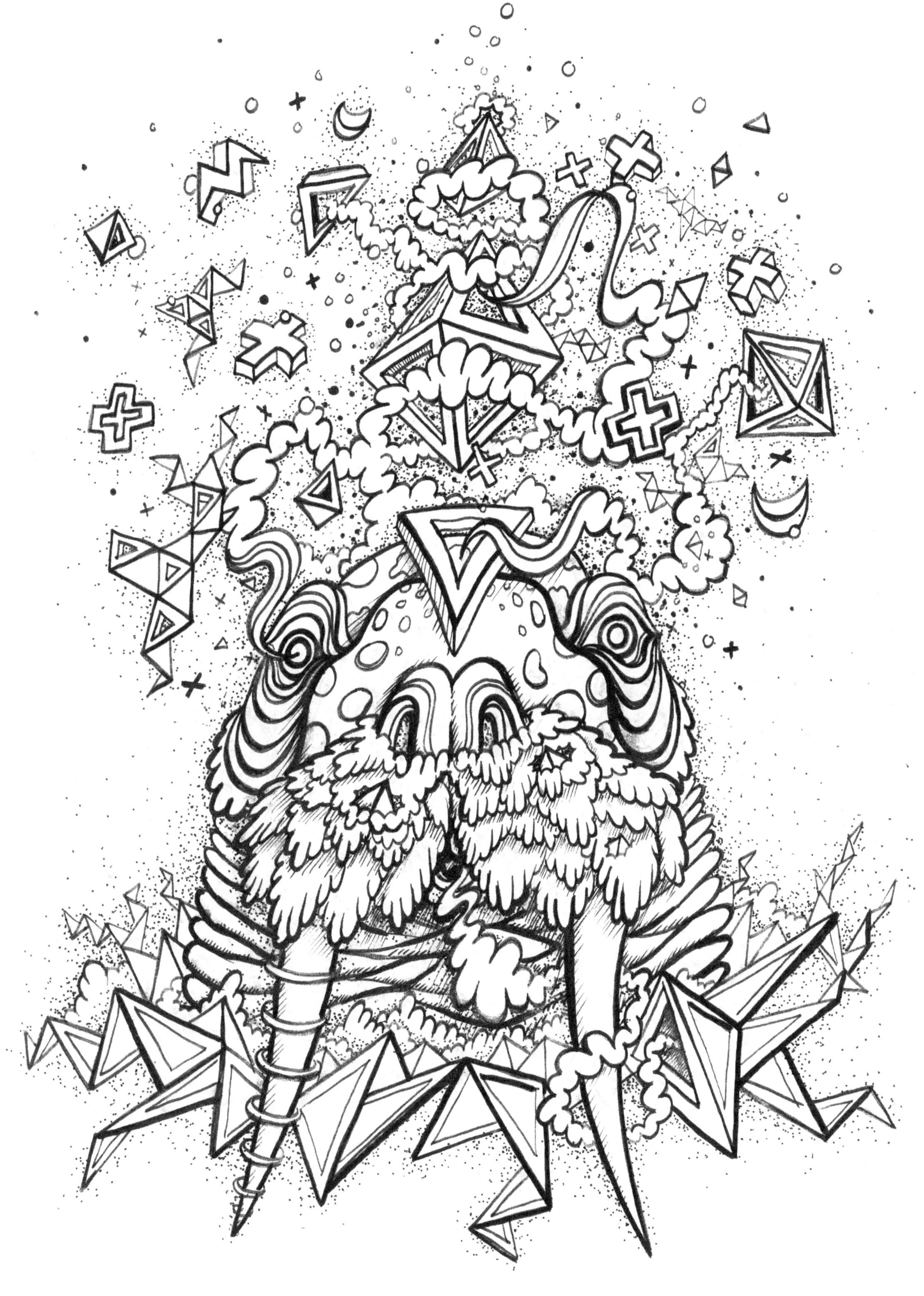

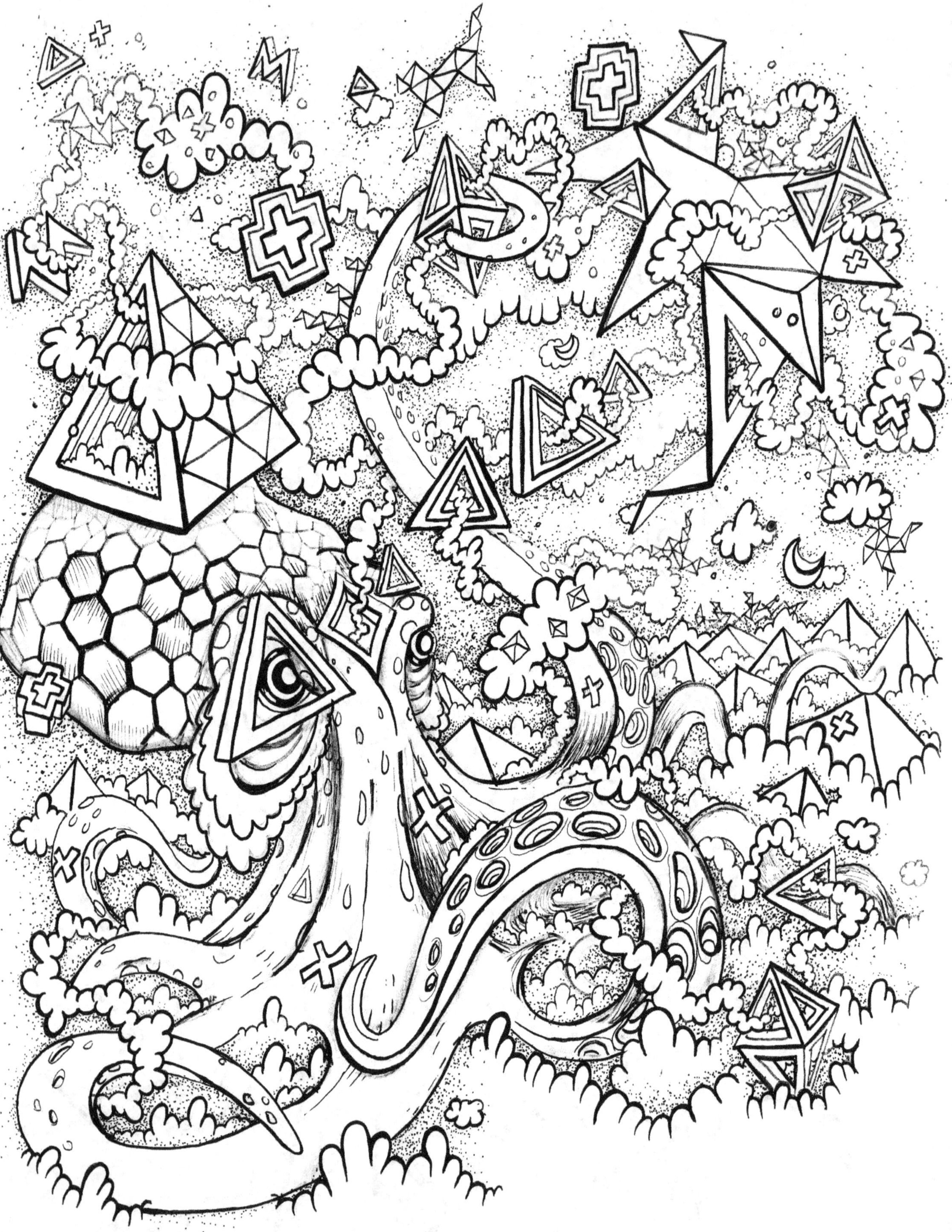

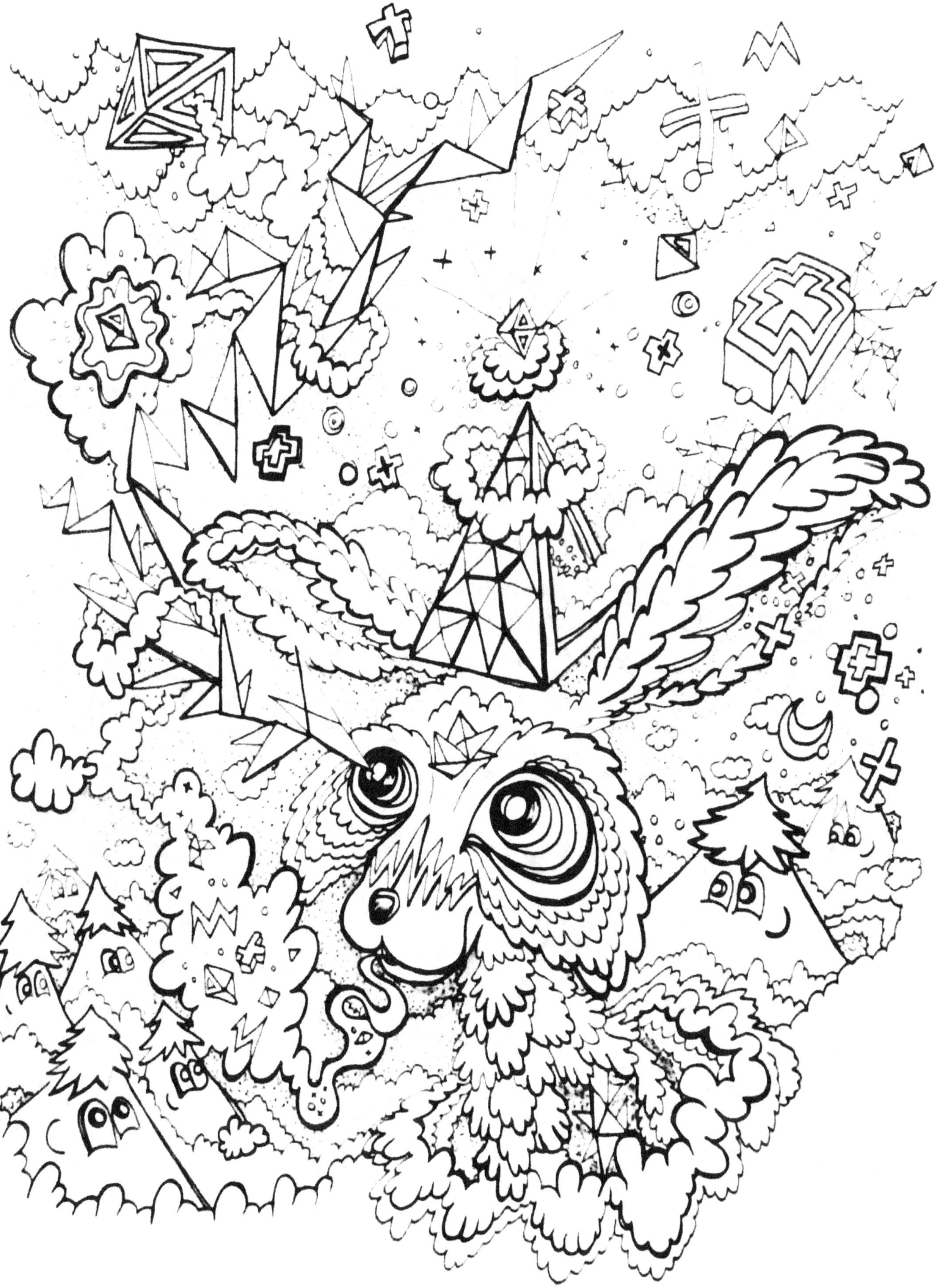

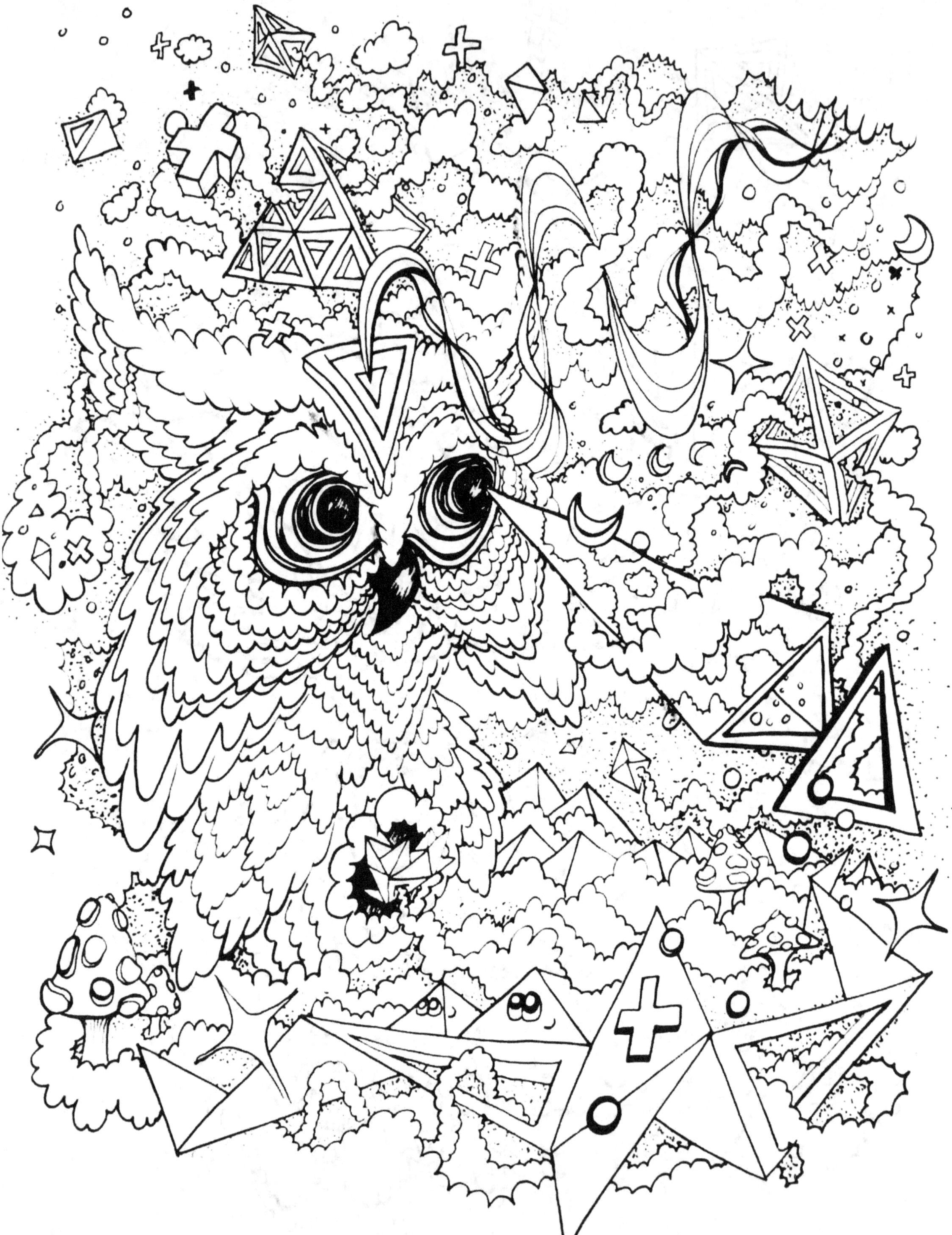

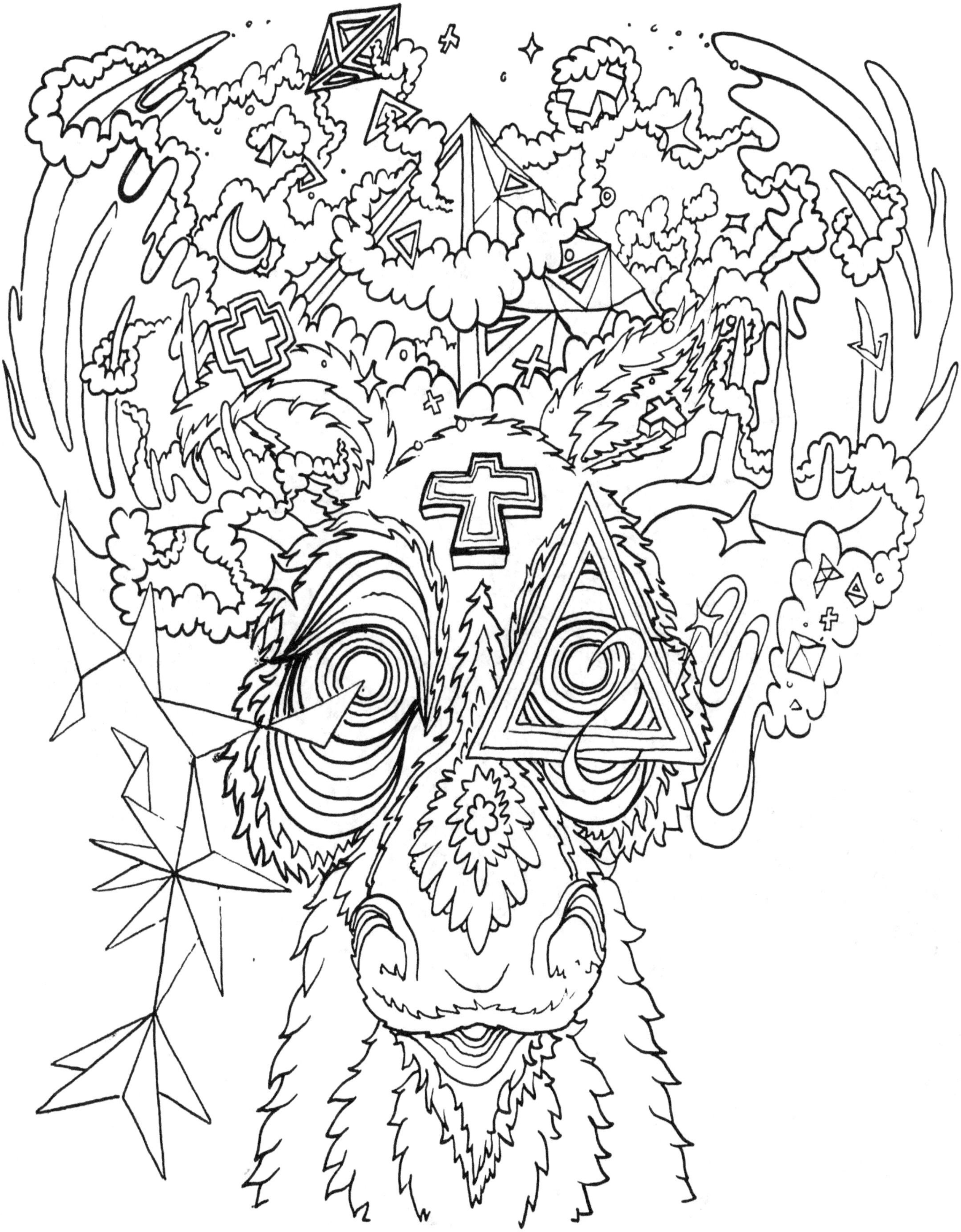

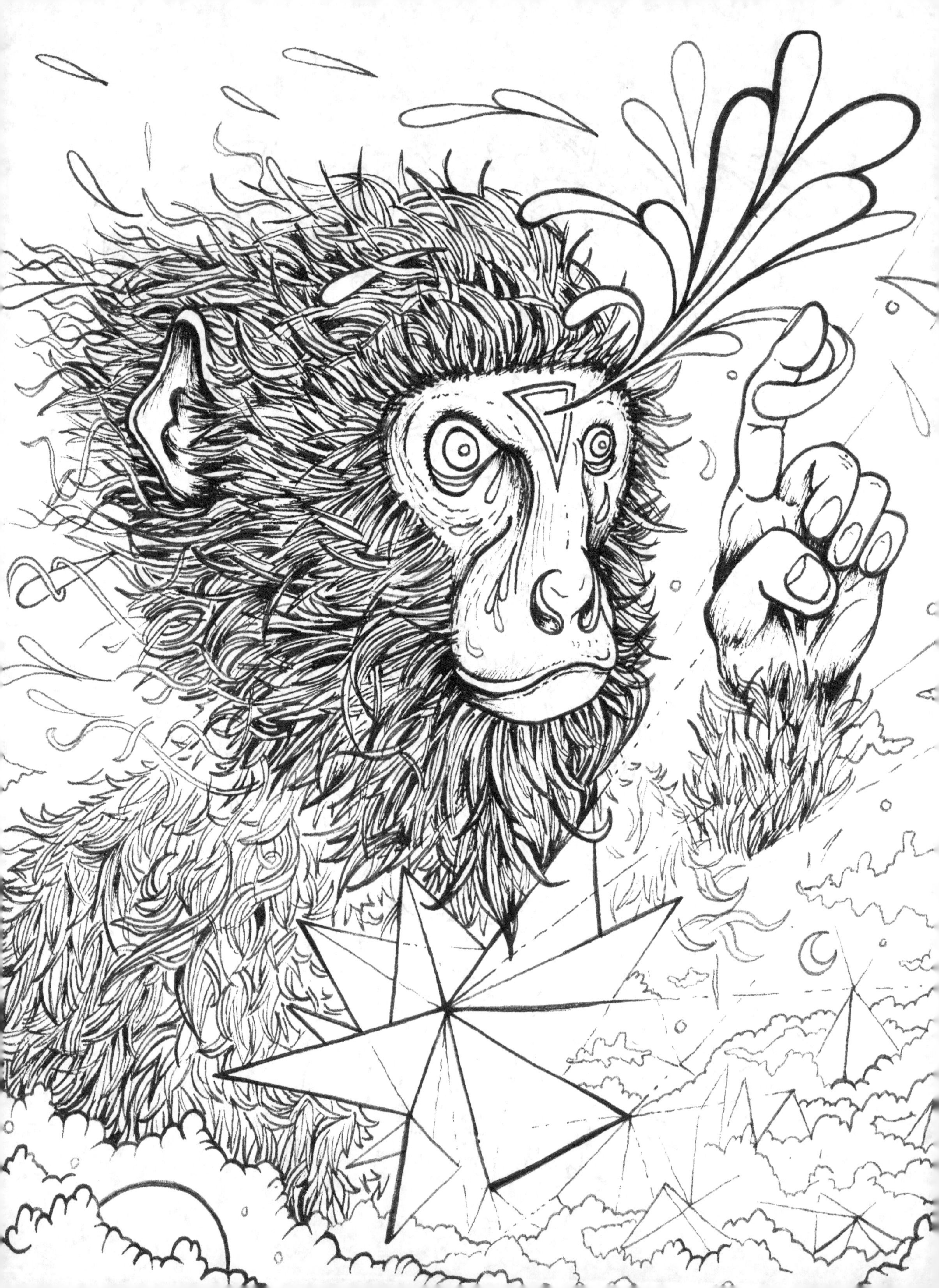

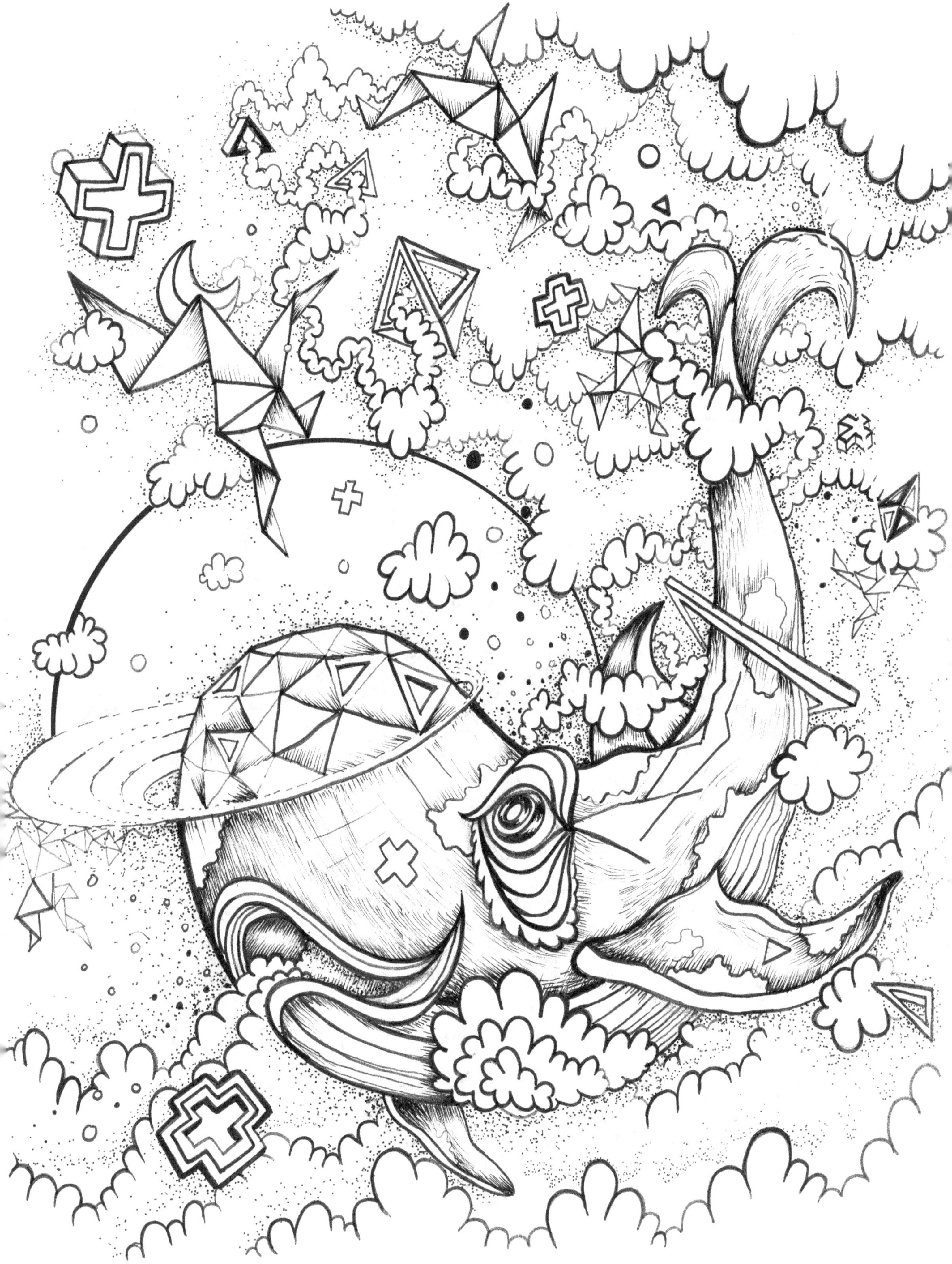

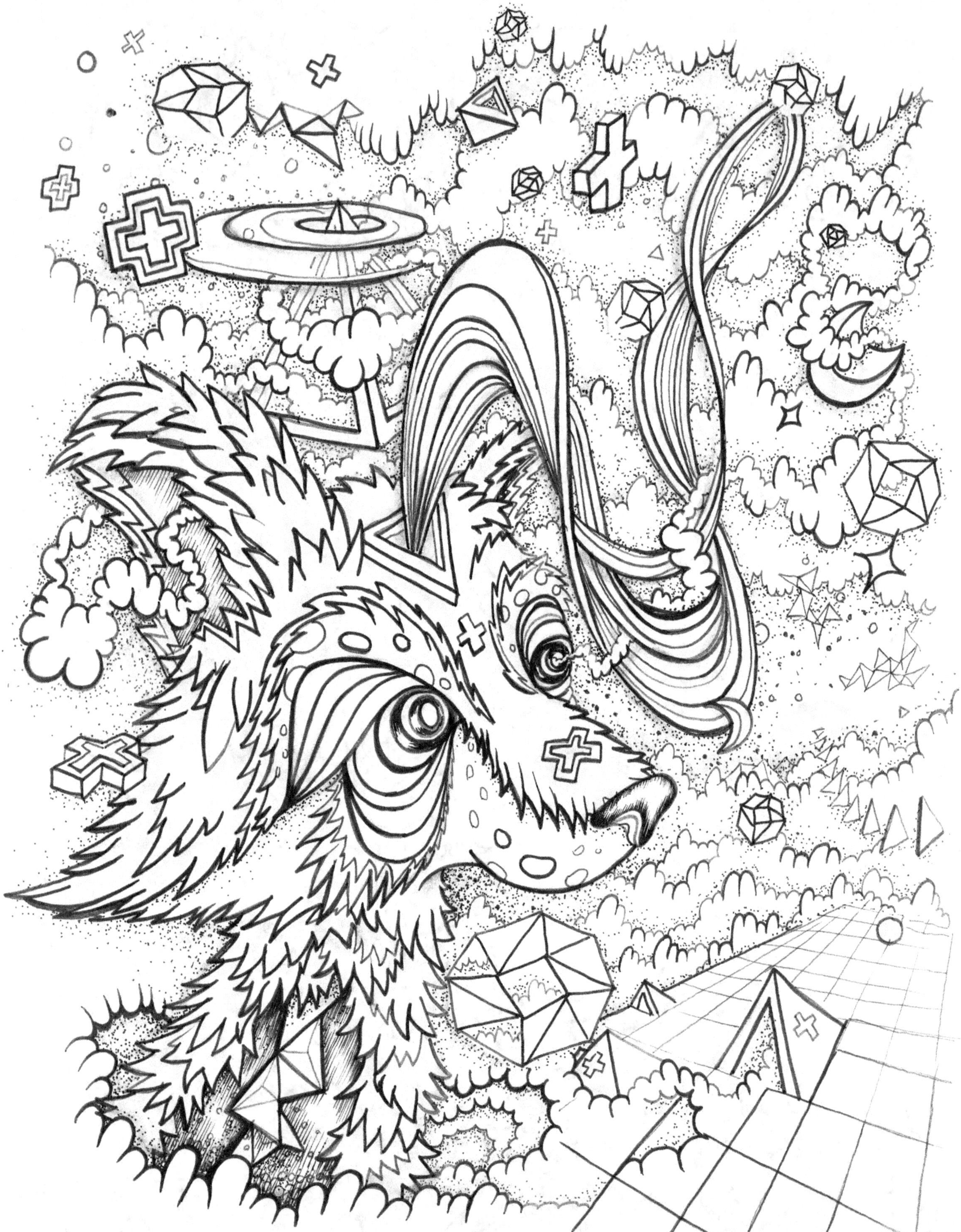

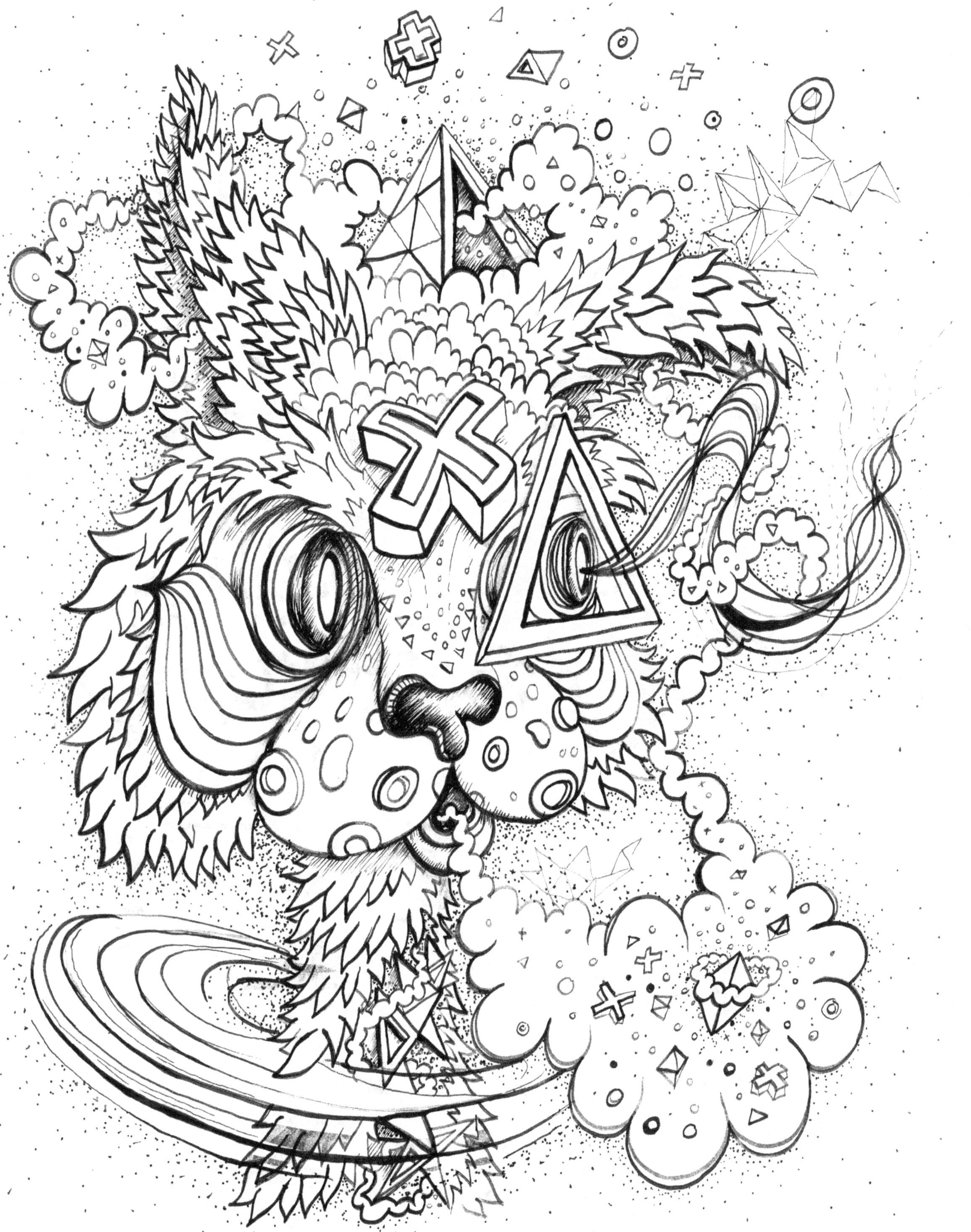

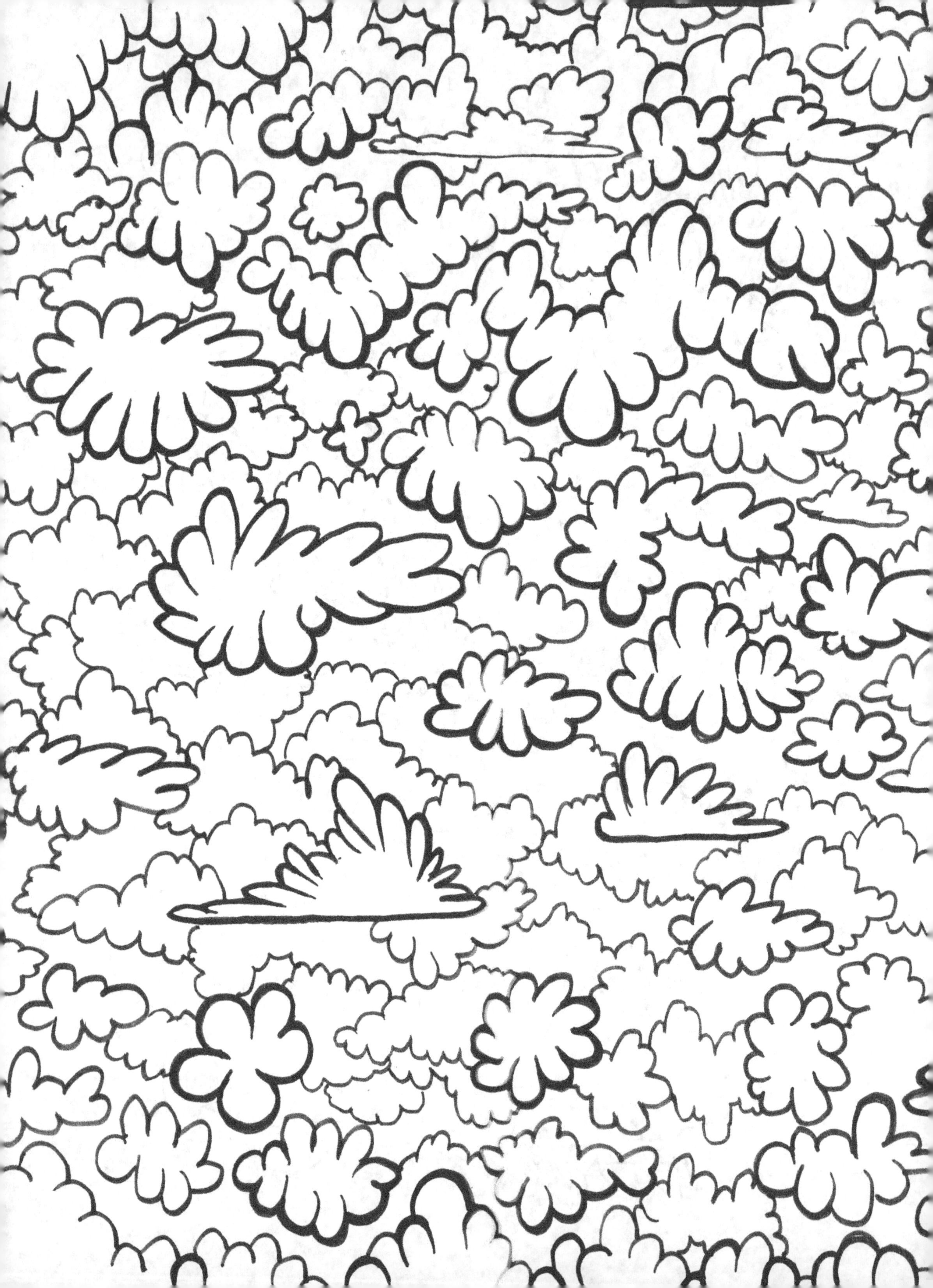

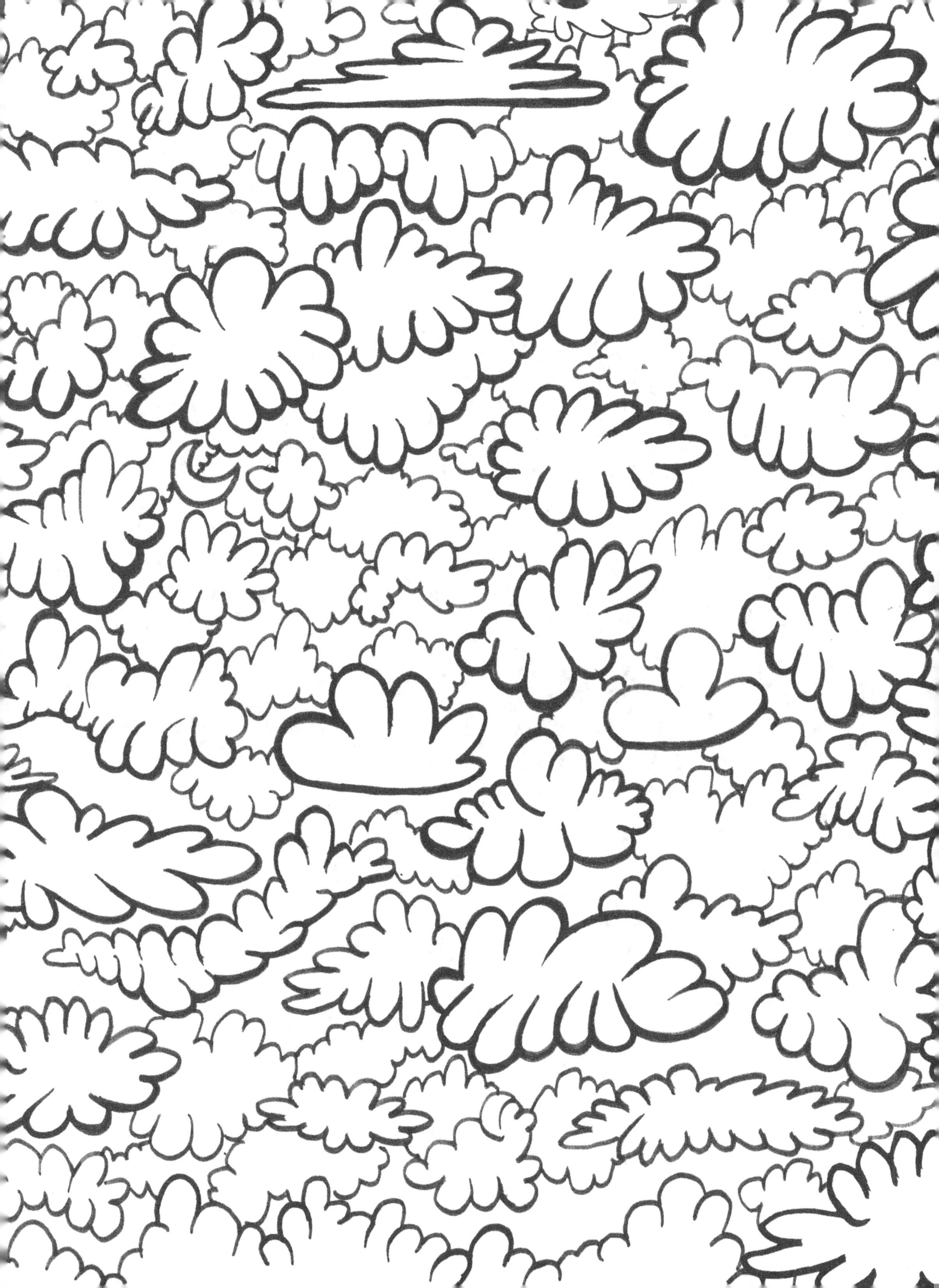

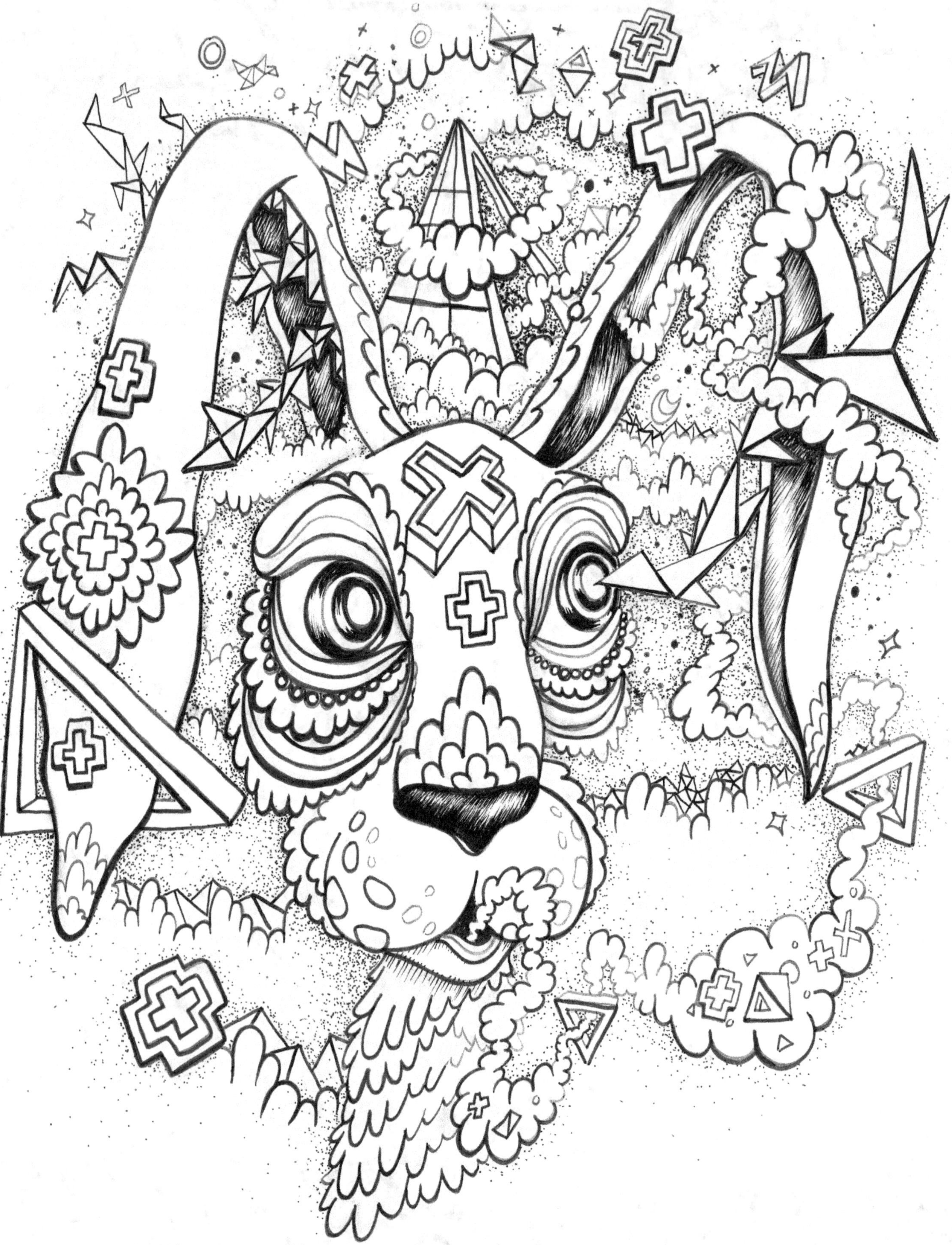

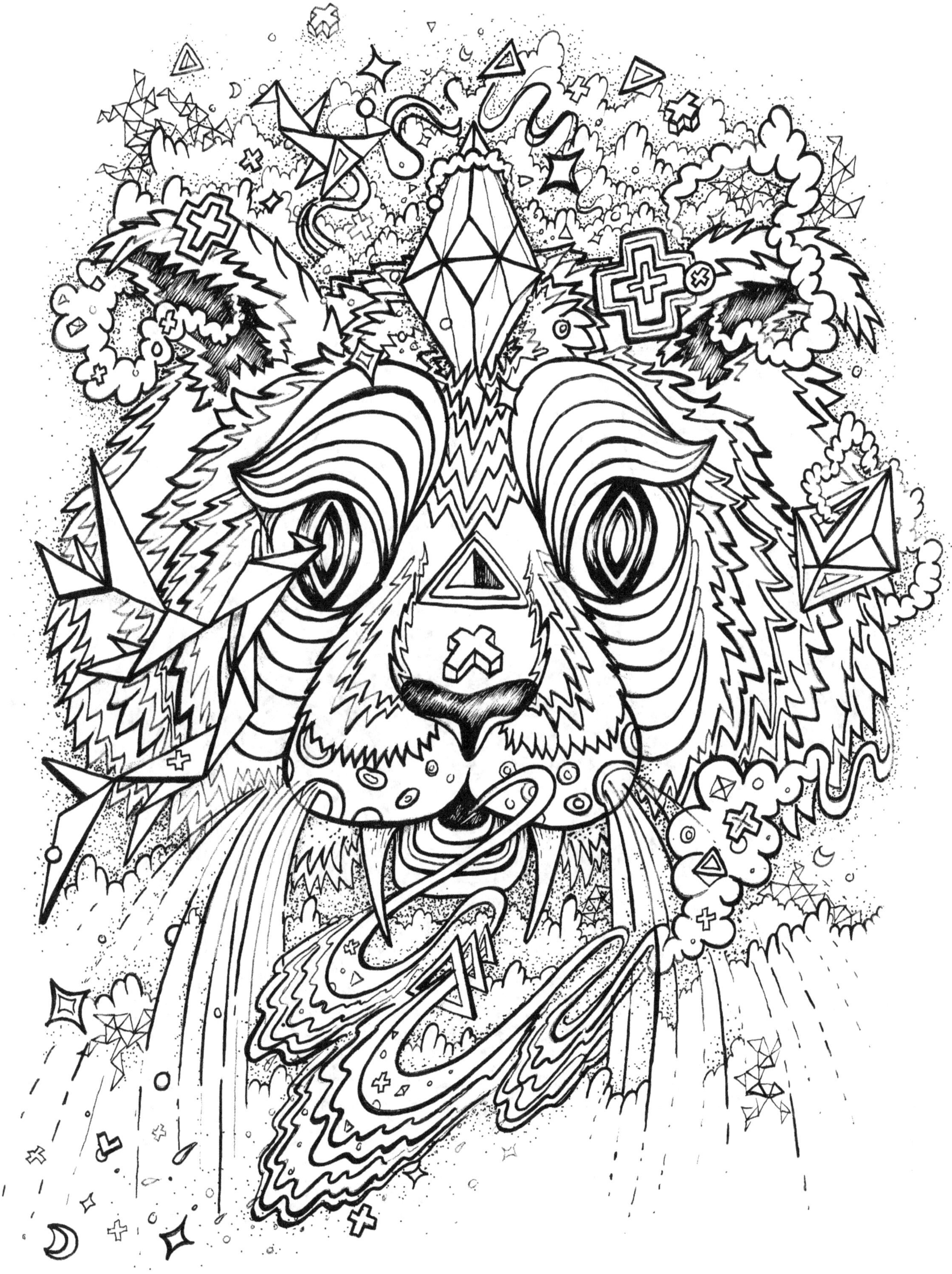

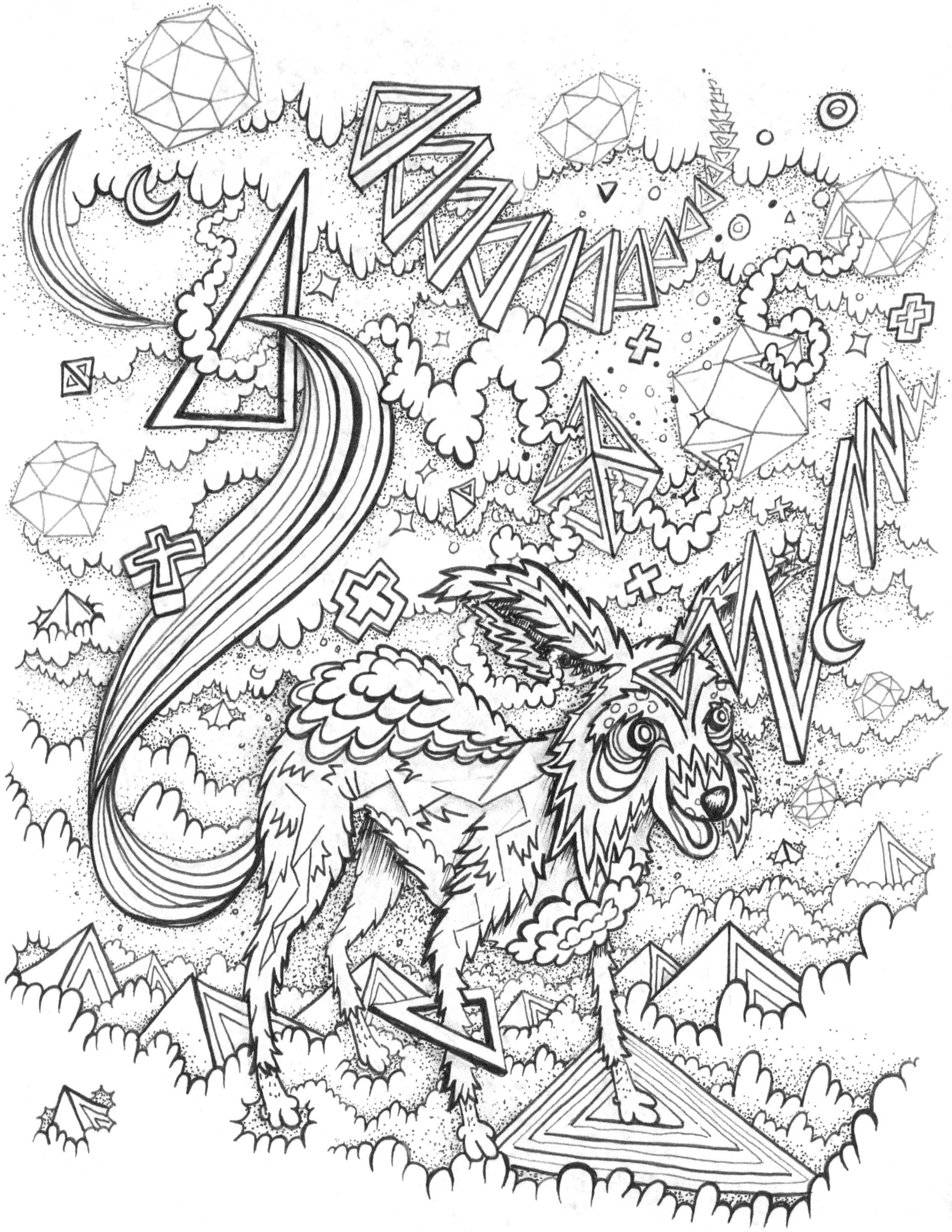

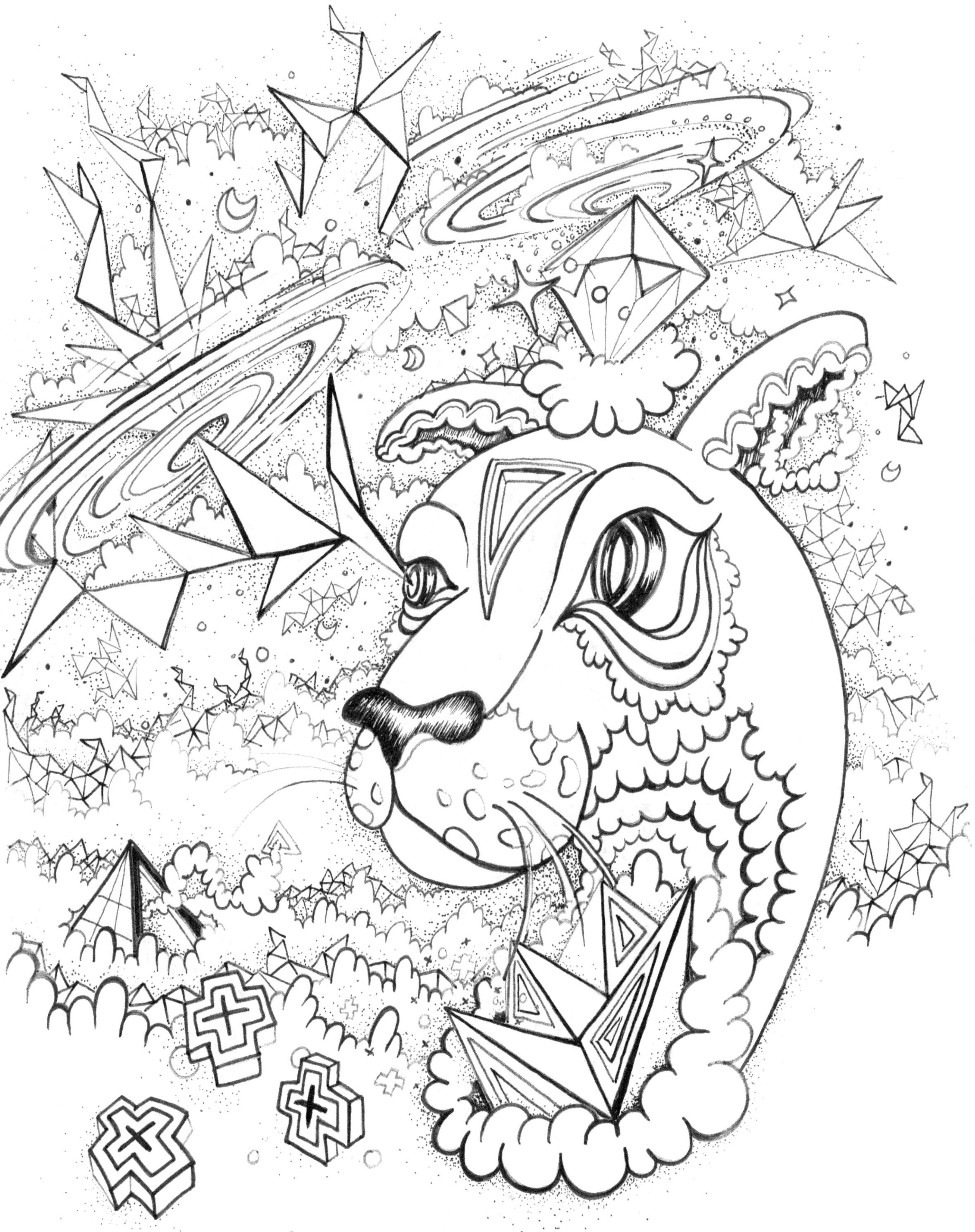

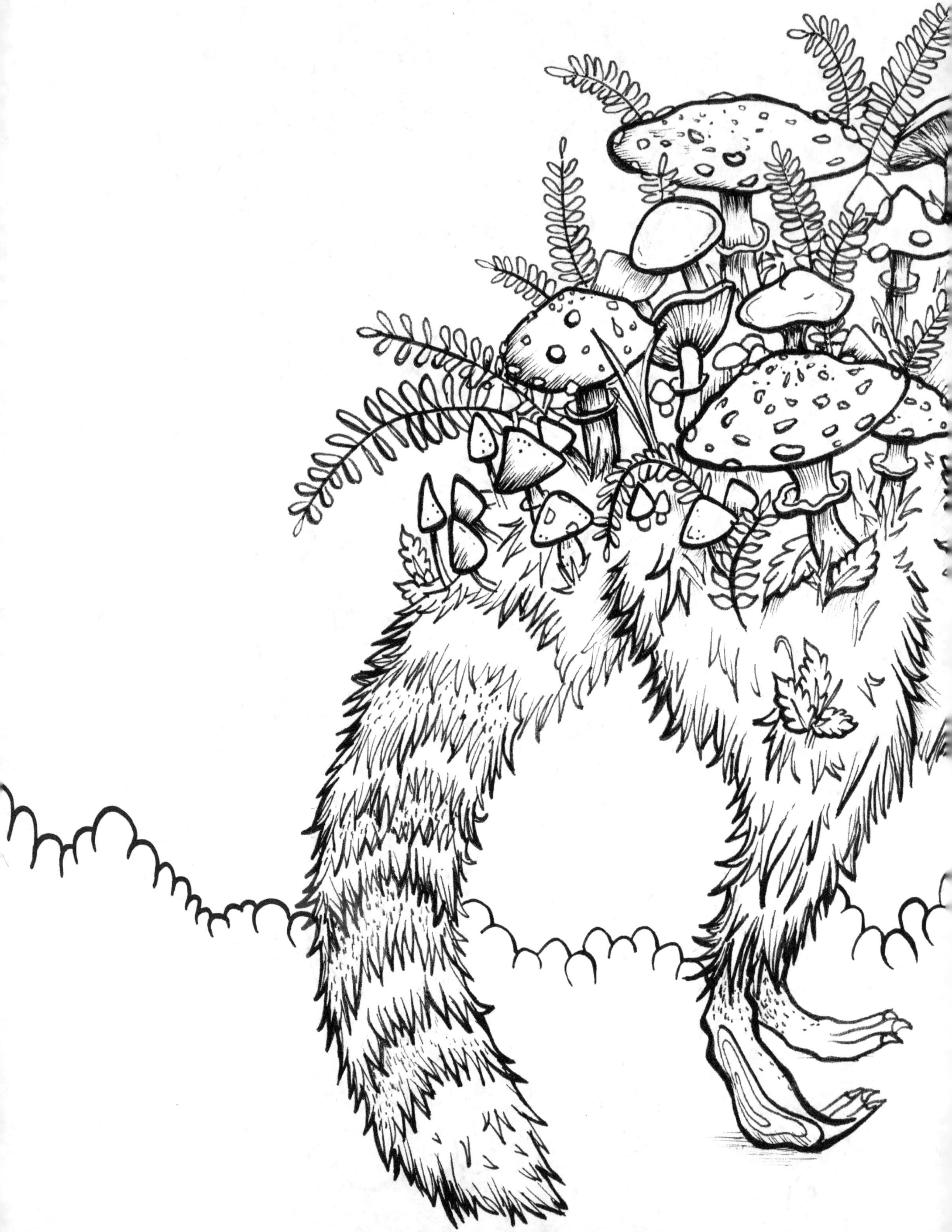

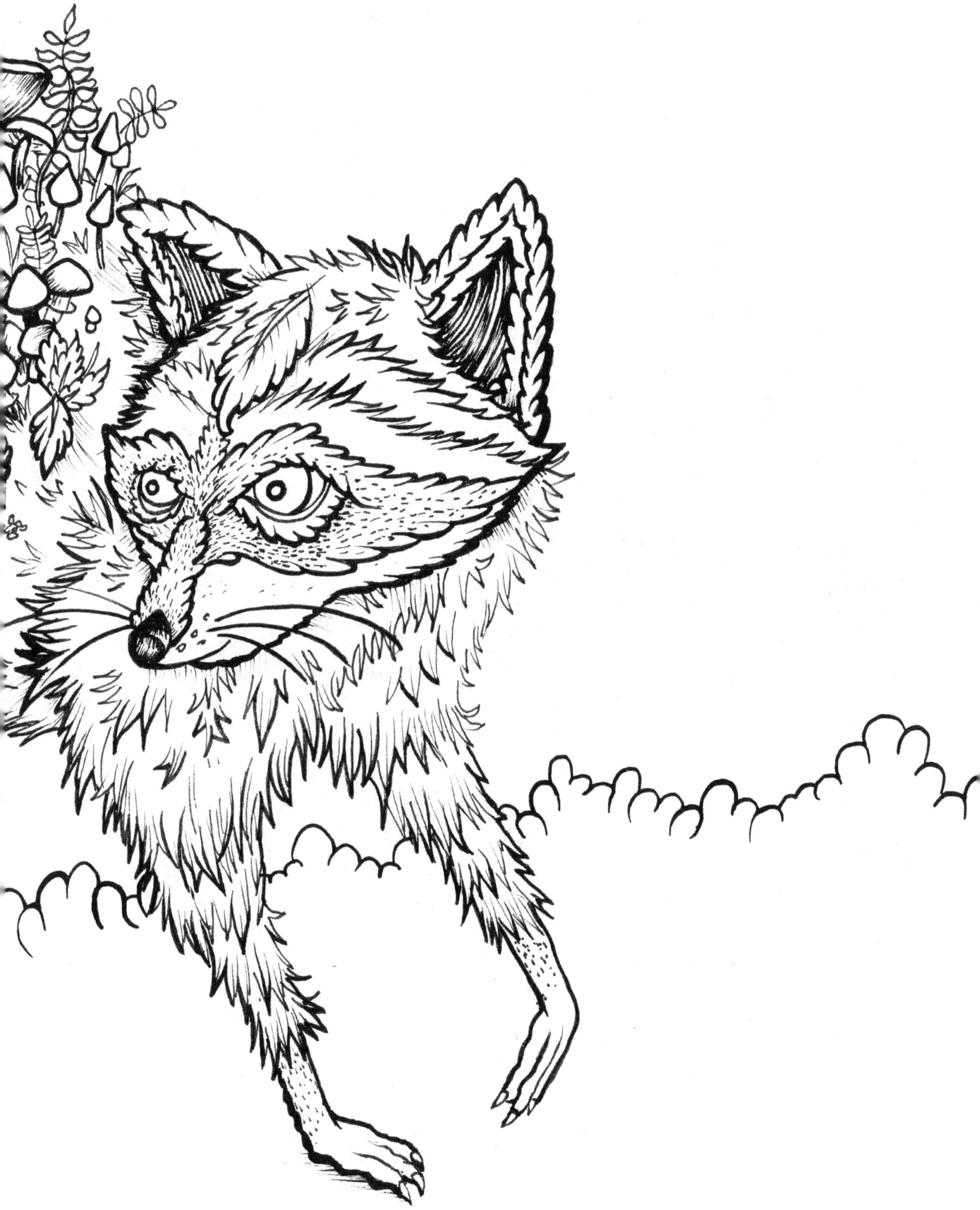

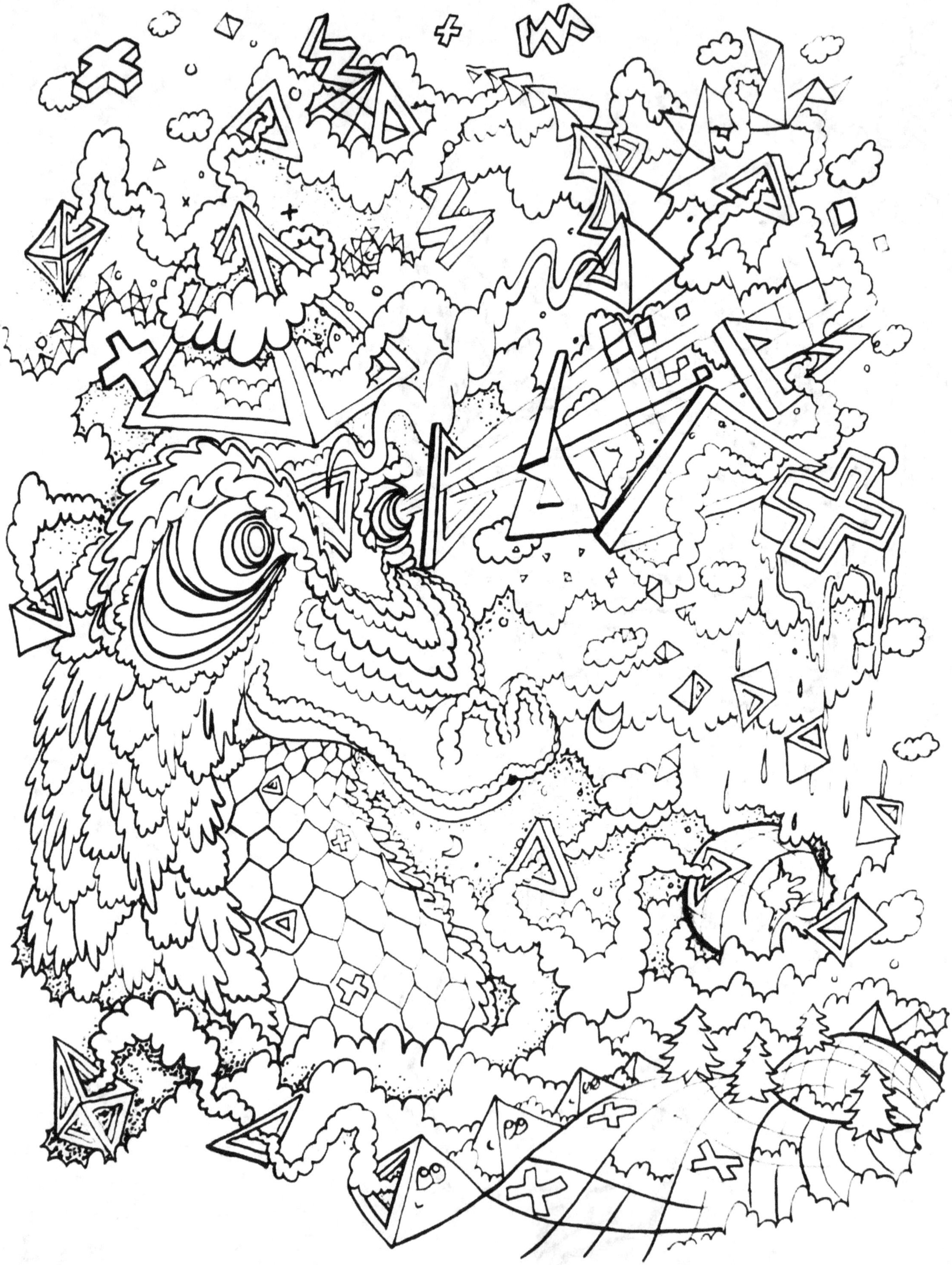

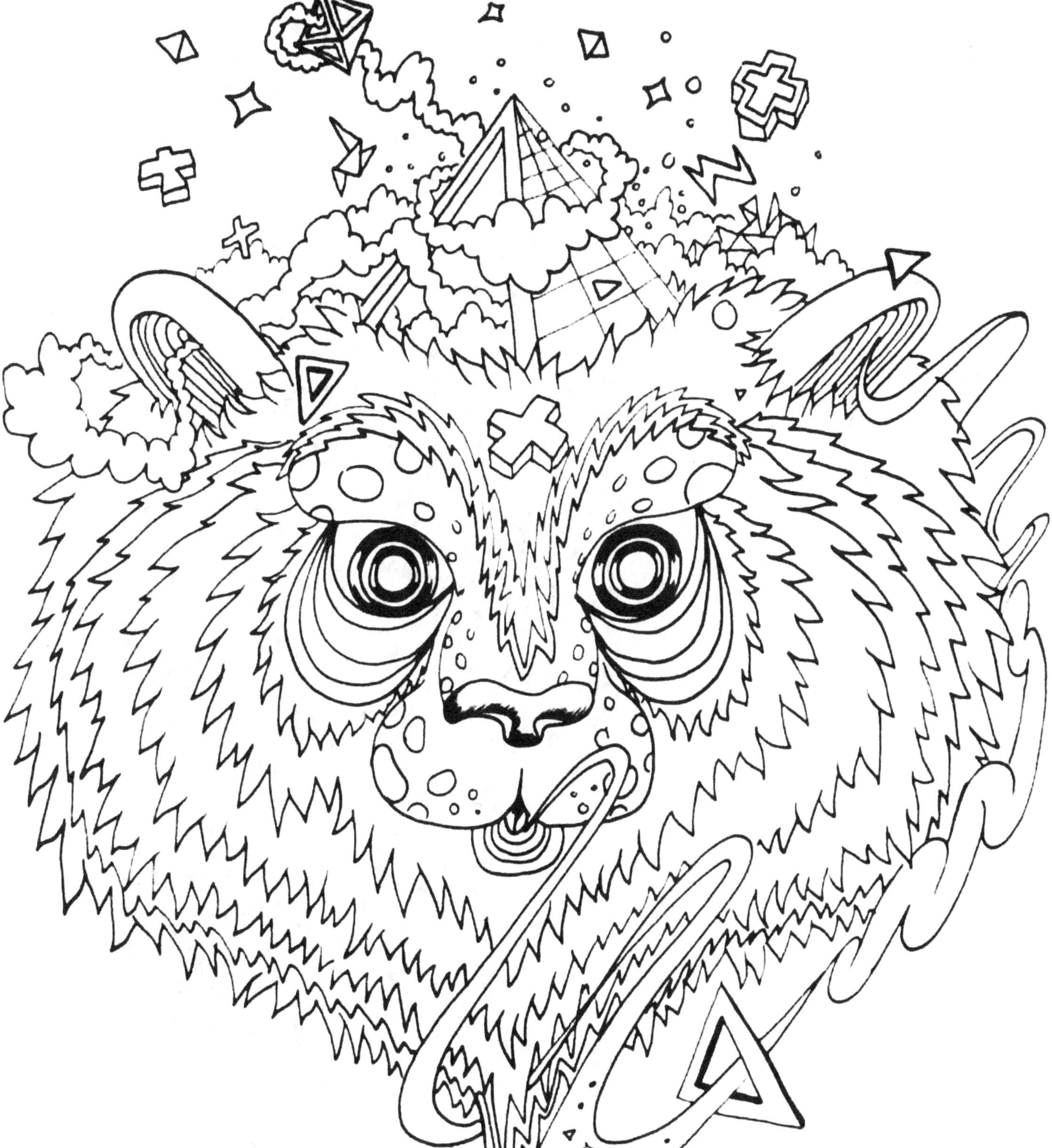

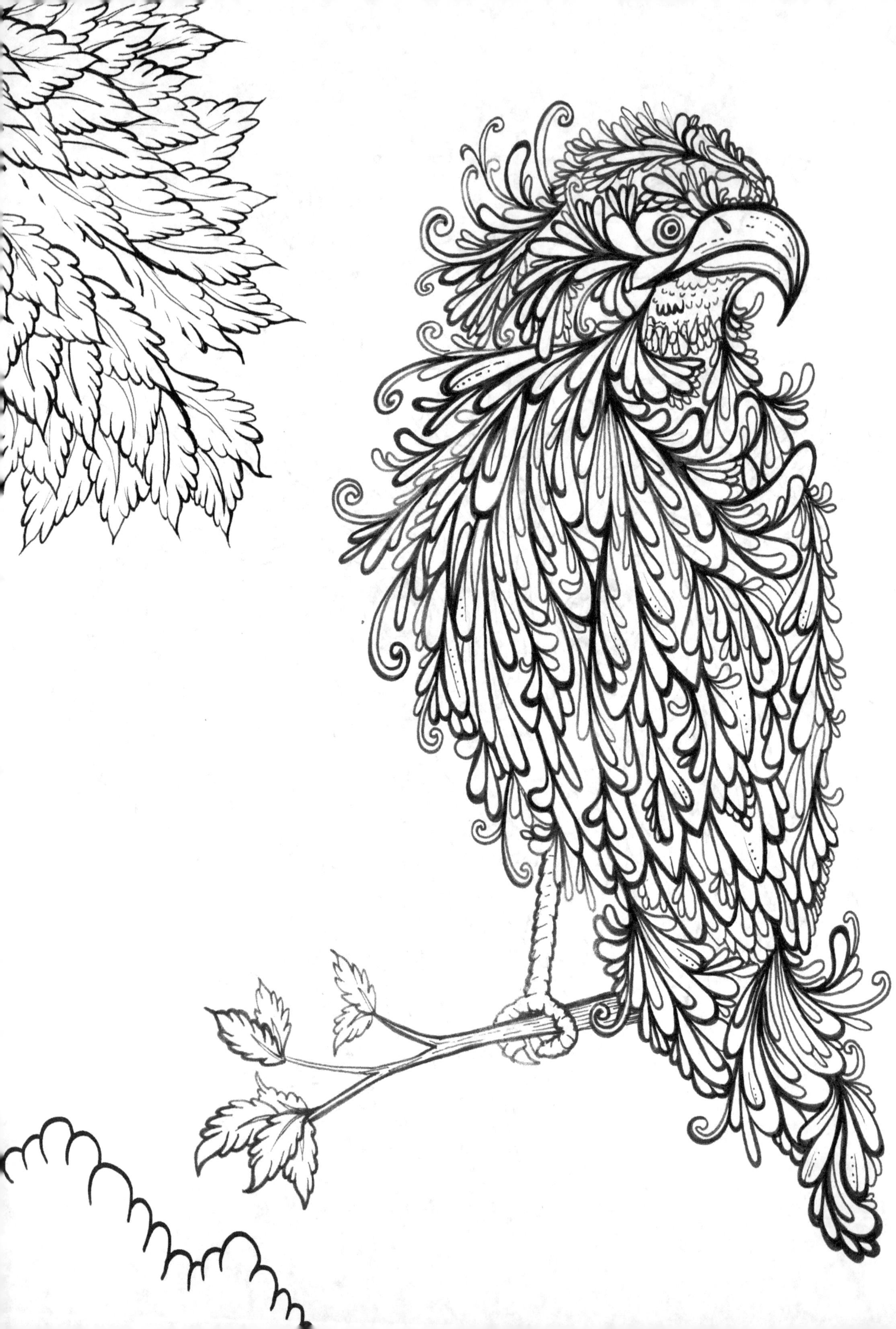

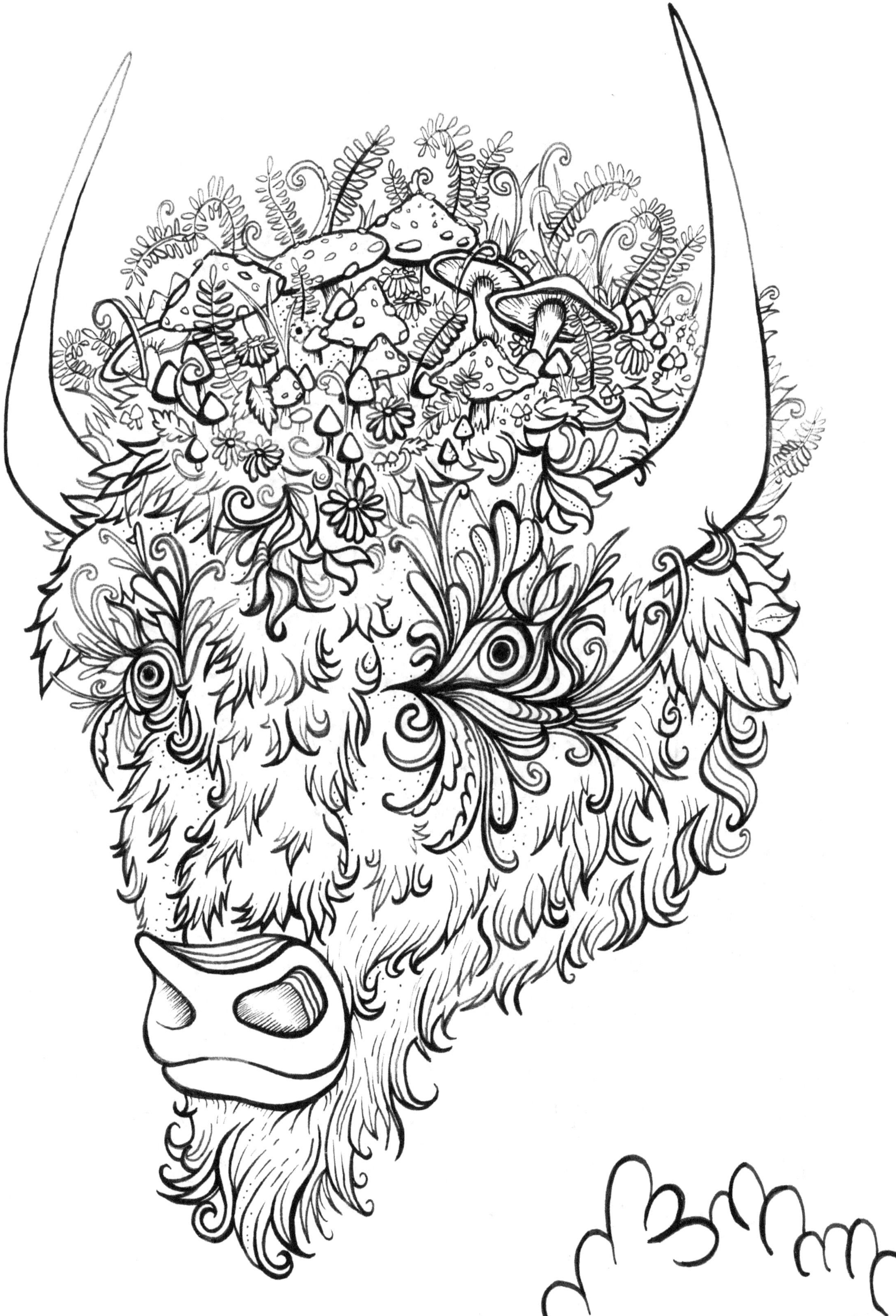

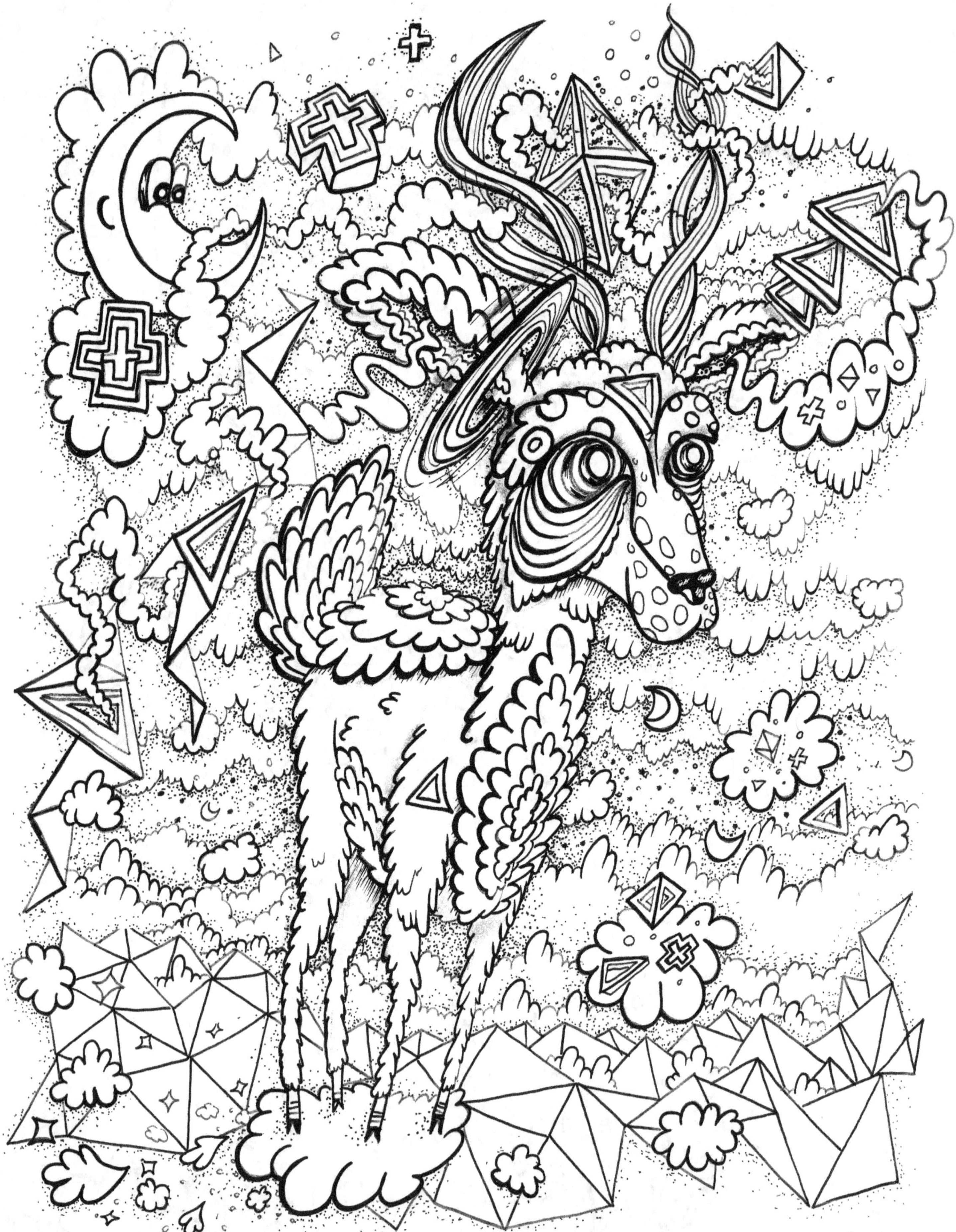

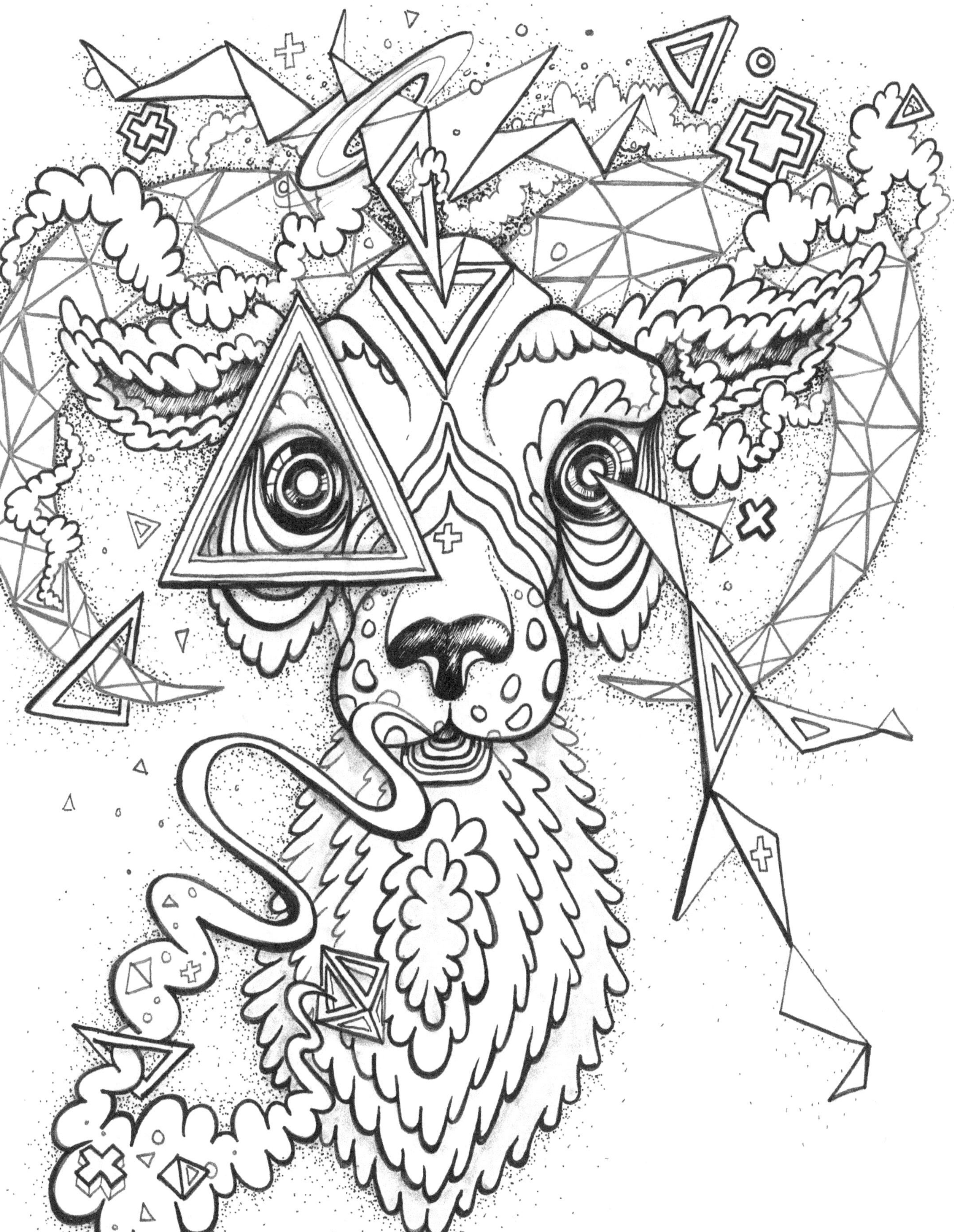

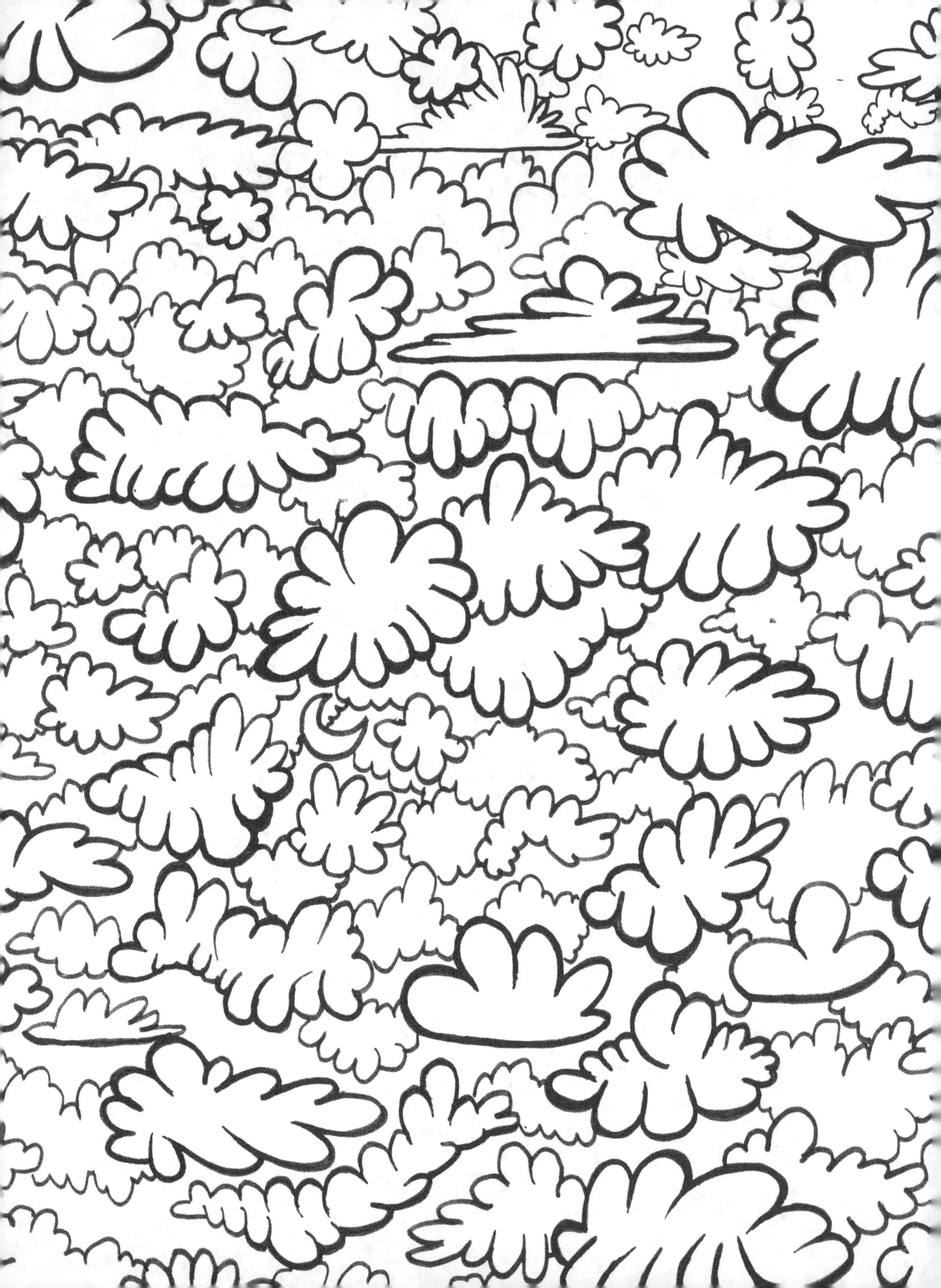

www.ingramcontent.com/pod-product-compliance
Lightning Source LLC
Chambersburg PA
CBHW082035190526
45165CB00020B/3225